The (Wonderful) Truth About Santa

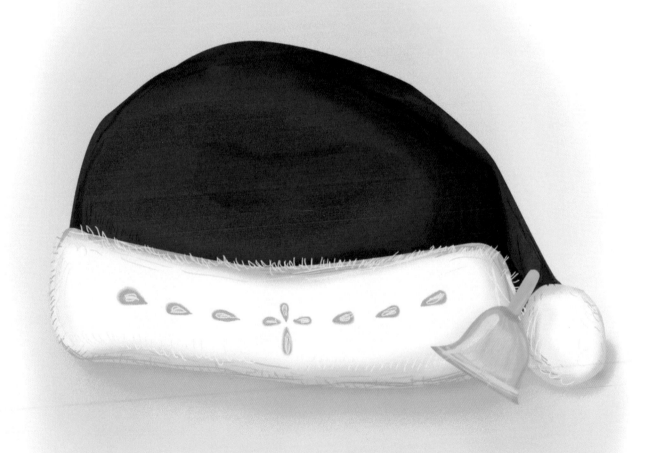

by B.K. Gendron

illustrated by Jess Jansen

THE (WONDERFUL) TRUTH ABOUT SANTA

ISBN: 978-0-9905928-3-9

Grandpa, is Santa real?

Sit on my lap and let me tell you a story.

Many years ago, there lived a kind and humble man named **Saint Nicholas.**

Saint Nicholas heard that there was a *very* poor family in his town.

They were in **desperate need**.

So one snowy night he snuck into their home and dropped gold coins into their stockings, which were drying by the fire.

He worked quickly and quietly hoping not to be seen,
but the father of the house **spotted him in the dark**.

Why didn't he want to be seen?

Saint Nicholas didn't want any credit or praise.
He knew that the **real gift** of giving was the *joy it gave to others*.

"Keep the coins, but tell no one who gave them to you,"
Saint Nicholas told the father.

Then what happened?

The father was **so grateful** he couldn't help himself.

He shared what happened with his neighbors and the good deeds of Saint Nicholas *spread far and wide*.

People everywhere were inspired to give **in secret**.

Hundreds of years passed and the legend of Saint Nicholas' generosity **continued to live on**.

People decided that every Christmas, when the weather outside was at its coldest, they would spread the **warmth of the holiday spirit** by giving in secret.

As people gave to one another,
they were warmed from the inside out like a *cup of hot cocoa*.

Parents realized how important it was to teach children about the spirit of giving, so every December, they told their little ones about Saint Nicholas, only they used a different name: **Santa Claus.**

They told their children about how he came in the night to the family in need and left coins in their stockings.

From then onwards, every Christmas Eve, as their little one's slept,
parents would fill their children's stockings with treats,
just like Saint Nicholas had.

Other parents left gifts for their children under the tree,
or in their shoes.

Remembering that Saint Nicholas refused to take credit for his good deeds, the parents told their children that the gifts were not from them, *but from Santa.*

That tradition continues to this day.

Why don't parents want kids to know the gifts are from them?

Because, that's what Saint Nicholas taught us.

Giving is not about taking credit, but about the *joy a gift brings.*

So, *who* is Santa?

Saint Nicholas was the first Santa Claus,
but anyone who shares the *spirit* of the holiday
through giving is a Santa.

Today there is more than just one.
The Santa at the mall spreads joy by filling children with **cheer**.

The Santa Claus you see taking donations
brings **comfort** and **joy** by providing for those in need.

There are also **secret Santas** who,
every holiday season, deliver presents.

They work quickly and quietly, never revealing their identities.

Do I have my own Santa?

Yes.
Every Christmas Eve, **parents around the world** are Santa Claus.

They continue the work of Saint Nicholas,
by leaving gifts for their sleeping children to **open when they wake**.

You see, that feeling you get in the morning when you see the presents, that's the *holiday spirit*.

It comes from your parents **giving to you**.

Now that it's in your heart, whenever you feel sad, even when you're a grown up, you'll only have to recall the magical Christmases of your youth to feel **joy** in your heart.

It's like a cup of hot cocoa that *never* **runs out**.

Should I tell other children the truth about Santa?

No. You must *never* blow out another child's Santa spark
before it has burned warm enough to last them a lifetime.

When they're ready, someone they love will tell them
who their Santa is.

One day, you'll have little ones of your own and it will be your turn to be their secret Santa Claus. But you don't have to wait until then.

I don't?

Now that you know the secret of Saint Nicholas,
you can give the spirit of the holiday to someone you love.

Choose one person and be their secret Santa.

And remember,
never stop believing because *Santa is everywhere.*

Dedicated to all who believe.

Printed in Great Britain
by Amazon